NISHNAWBE

A Story of Indians in Michigan

By Lynne Deur

Illustrated with maps,
photos, old prints,
and drawings
by
Lori McElrath

RIVER ROAD PUBLICATIONS, INC.

CREDITS

The illustrations are reproduced through the courtesy of: pp. cover, opp. 1, 2, 4, 8, 15, 18, 19, 21 (top), 24, 25, 33, 35, Lori McElrath; p. 7, Milwaukee Public Museum; pp. 12, 40, Michigan State Archives; pp. 13, 14, 23, American Museum of Natural History; p. 16, National Museum of Natural History, Smithsonian Institution; p. 21, National Anthropological Archives, Smithsonian Institution; p. 26, Field Museum of Natural History, Chicago; p. 28, Museum of the American Indian, Heye Foundation; p. 37, McCord Museum, McGill University, Montreal; p. 41, Northern Indiana Historical Society; pp. 44, 48, Grand Rapids Inter-Tribal Council.

COPYRIGHT

Published by River Road Publications, Inc. Spring Lake, Michigan 49456

ISBN: 0-938682-00-8 / paperbound
Library of Congress catalog card number 81-508838

CONTENTS

NISHNAWBE
A STORY OF INDIANS IN MICHIGAN

Nishnawbe (nish NAW bey) is a word used by Michigan Indians to mean "Indian." For thousands of years Indians lived along the rivers and lakes and in the huge forests of the land we now call Michigan. Their story stretches across these years, a time when no other people in the world knew about this beautiful place. It is a story of struggle with people from Europe who found the land and wanted to make it their own. It is a story of sadness as Indians lost their homes and lands to settlers. It is also a story that goes on today . . . as Indian people try to keep the best of their past alive.

Indians lived in the Michigan area thousands of years before any other people in the world knew about this place.

The first Indians

Thousands of years ago there were no recorded histories as there are today. These years of unwritten history are called prehistory. We do know some things about people and their way of life during these years, however. This is because men and women called archaeologists (are key OL o jests) dig to find traces of the past. They study bones, broken tools, spearheads, and other remains to discover how the first Indians lived.

Archaeologists have learned that Indians lived in the land we now call Michigan for more than 10,000 years. This was so long ago that glaciers* still covered part of the area around the Great Lakes. Huge beasts that no longer live on earth walked the land. Some of these animals were mammoths,* mastodons,* and a giant kind of beaver.

Mammoths once roamed the area that we know today as southern Michigan.

*See glossary.

3

The first Indians did not settle down and live in one area. Instead they moved from place to place and very likely hunted the huge animals for food. Spearheads used by these first Indian hunters have been found in the state. In many southern counties bones of mastodons have also been discovered, sometimes by farmers plowing their fields!

As thousands of years passed, changes slowly took place. The weather became warmer and new kinds of trees and plants grew. The huge beasts died and smaller kinds of animals replaced them. Moose, bear, and deer roamed the land instead of mammoths and mastodons.

The Indians themselves changed. They learned to use boats. They began to fish and gather berries, nuts, and plants to eat. In what is now Michigan's Upper Peninsula, Indians dug copper from rich mines and shaped it into useful tools. As time went by, life became a little easier than it had been for the very first hunters.

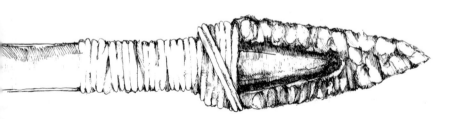

A spear used by an early Indian hunter may have looked something like this one.

The Hopewell people

In what is now the southern and middle United States lived a people who were well-known for building mounds. Inside these large piles of earth they buried their dead. They also buried tools, jewelry, and weapons for their dead. Many of the mound-building people were later named Hopewell Indians.

Some of the mound-building Hopewells came to live in what is now Michigan. They settled along the Grand River where Grand Rapids is today. The Grand River Hopewells built between 45 and 55 mounds. Some of the mounds were about as big as a school bus. Others were bigger than a two-story house! Hopewell people also settled along the Muskegon and Saginaw rivers. Archaeologists think that Hopewell people lived in these Michigan areas for about 700 years (see the chart on page 11).

The Hopewell way of life was a step ahead of most Indian groups of the time. Just building the mounds took planning and hard work. When they dug into the mounds, archaeologists discovered that the Hopewells made fine sculptures, masks, bowls, tools, and carved pipes. The archaeologists also found a kind of cloth. After studying it carefully, they decided that the Hopewells twisted stringy material which grows inside certain tree barks to make thread for the cloth.

Some of the things found inside the mounds told archaeologists that the Hopewell people traded their goods with Indians in distant places. In Michigan mounds were conch* shells from the Gulf of Mexico. There were things

THE FIRST COPPER MINERS

Over five thousand years ago Indians mined copper in what is now Michigan's Upper Peninsula.

Long, long ago—even before the time of Moses in the Bible—Indians discovered copper in what is now Michigan's Upper Peninsula. What a discovery it must have been! After depending on stone for their tools and weapons, the Indians found a metal that could be pounded into many shapes and would not crack.

The first Indian miners also discovered a way to get to the larger beds of copper which lay under the earth. They built fires and heated the rocks that covered the copper. Then they quickly poured cold water over the hot rock to crack it. Deep in the cracks they dug out the copper-filled rock. Slowly they made deep mining pits.

As time went by, thousands of mining pits were made by Indians. They shaped the copper into knives, spearheads, axes, and other tools. They also traded it with Indians from other areas who probably thought very highly of these early miners. Upper Peninsula copper has been found all over the United States, in Mexico, and Central America.

The old, old copper mines have raised many questions. Who were these first miners? How did they discover copper?

Many of their tools were left in the mines in a way that looked as if they had gone home for the evening and expected to return the next day. Why did the miners leave? Why didn't other Indian tribes continue the work of the early miners? Such questions many never be answered. Experts know very little about these copper-mining people.

made of copper from Upper Peninsula mines. These mines were far away from Hopewell settlements. A pipe carved like an alligator was also found. No Hopewell artist in the Michigan area would have known about alligators.

The Hopewells hunted and fished, but they also depended on farming for much of their food. They were probably the very first people in the Michigan area to do so. Experts say that the Hopewells may have grown such crops as corn, squash, beans, and tobacco.

What happened to the Hopewell people? This is a secret of the past. Experts say that the Hopewell way of life may have ended because of a terrible sickness, famine,* or war with other people. Perhaps the secret will never be discovered.

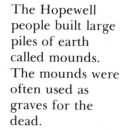

The Hopewell people built large piles of earth called mounds. The mounds were often used as graves for the dead.

Michigan's many Indian tribes

After the Hopewell way of life ended, another kind of Indian life began to unfold. Slowly the Indian people began to live in ways we most often read and learn about today. This stretch of time lasted about 800 years.

The history of Indians during these 800 years is not a simple one. Indian people belonged to different tribes, or groups. The people in a tribe shared the same language and ways of life. One tribe of Indians did not live together in a single place, however. A smaller group, or band, from one tribe might live hundreds of miles from another band of the same tribe. They might move to find better hunting or fishing. At other times they might be driven away from an area because of battles with Indians of another tribe. Through the years Indians from a number of different tribes made their homes in what is now Michigan.

When explorers and traders from Europe came to the Michigan area, three main groups of Indians lived here. These were the Ottawa, the Potawatomi (pot a WAT o me), and the Ojibwa (o JIB wa), often called the Chippewa. People of other tribes also lived in the area at one time or another. They were from the Miami, Huron, Mascouten (mas COO ten), and Menominee (men OM i nee) tribes.

UNDERSTANDING TIME AND HISTORY

When we learn about history, we often read and hear about things that took place 100 or 200 years ago. That is very young history! Time reaches back thousands and thousands of years!

In our world today we measure time and history by the beginning of the Christian religion, or birth of Jesus Christ. Years before Christ was born are called B.C. Those after are called A.D. As the time chart shows, Indian people lived in North America thousands of years before Jesus Christ was born in another part of the world.

Indian people kept histories in their own ways. Still, we call the time the Indians lived alone in North America prehistory. The years after people began coming from Europe are called history. For this reason there are many years of prehistory in North America and only a few hundred years of history.

■ Years of history

☐ Years of prehistory

Life in Other Parts of the World		Indian Life in Michigan Area
	10,000 B.C.	
	9,000 B.C.	Early Indian people are already in Michigan area Mastodons & other huge animals roam the land
	8,000 B.C.	
	7,000 B.C.	
	6,000 B.C.	
	5,000 B.C.	
	4,000 B.C.	Indians mine copper in what is now the Upper Peninsula
People of Egypt begin building pyramids	3,000 B.C.	
Moses leads people of Israel	2,000 B.C.	
First known Olympic game	1,000 B.C.	
Vikings sail to North America	Birth of Jesus Christ	Time of the Hopewells
Settlers come to America	1,000 A.D.	Indians live in ways we usually study today
The 1980s & 1990s		Indians lose their lands to settlers

Some tribes were related to others. The Ojibwa, Ottawa, and Potawatomi had many things in common. They lived much like all Indians in what is now the northeastern United States. Their languages were different in some ways, but in other ways they were like a main language called Algonquian (al GON quee an). Sometimes the three tribes came together in times of trouble. They were often called the Three Fires.

Arrowheads and other objects used by Indian people help archaeologists discover some of the secrets of the past.

The Ojibwa

Villages of Indian people called Ojibwa were spread over a very large area. There were many in what is now northern Michigan and southern Canada. Still other villages were in the present states of Wisconsin, Minnesota, and North Dakota. The Ojibwa tribe was made up of so many different people, they could hardly be called a single tribe.

The Ojibwa had several different names. They called themselves Anissinape (AH nis si NAH bey), meaning Indian or person. Other Indian tribes called them Ojibwa. Early French explorers first came upon a group of Ojibwa fishing in the rapids where Sault Ste. Marie is today. For this reason the French called them Saulteurs (soo TER), or "people of the rapids." The name Chippewa was given to them by people who spoke English.

Ojibwa people built handsome birchbark canoes to use for hunting, fishing, and traveling.

The Ojibwa were greatly respected by other Indian tribes. They made handsome birchbark canoes which allowed them to travel quickly on rivers and lakes. They were good hunters, trappers, and fishermen. In times of war, they were also strong fighters.

The Ojibwa had plenty of meat and fish to eat, but they liked other foods too. In very early spring they gathered sap from maple trees. Then they boiled the sap until it turned to delicious maple sugar. In summer and fall they gathered nuts and berries. Some groups of Ojibwa harvested wild rice that grew in quiet, shallow waters of lakes, rivers, and streams. Groups who lived where the soil and weather were good for farming raised vegetables such as corn and squash.

Wild rice was an important food for Indian people living in the northern Michigan area. Here Ojibwa women beat the rice stalks and let the ripe grain fall into their canoes.

Ojibwa lived in houses called wigwams. Usually a wigwam was shaped like a bowl turned upside down. Its frame was made of bent poles. It might be covered with birchbark, animal skins, or woven mats. Sometimes wigwams were shaped like cones. The cone-shaped wigwams were often made with poles and bark. A fire was kept in the center of all wigwams. An Indian family slept around the fire using piles of warm furs for beds and blankets.

Like many other Indian peoples, the Ojibwa moved from time to time. Usually they made their homes near rivers and lakes where they could fish. In winter when food became hard to find they moved into the forests to hunt and trap. They built sturdy snowshoes and toboggans for traveling in the deep snow.

A wigwam was the most common type of house built by Indians in the Michigan area and was covered with bark, woven mats, or animal skins.

Both Ojibwa men and women were proud of the beautiful things they made. Shirts, moccasins, and bags were made from soft deerskin and decorated with porcupine quills. Drums, canoes, and birchbark buckets usually had handsome paintings on them. Ojibwa men carved war clubs, pipes, and cradleboards to hold babies. Many articles made by Ojibwa people are now kept in museums. They are important to understanding the past, as well as being fine works of art.

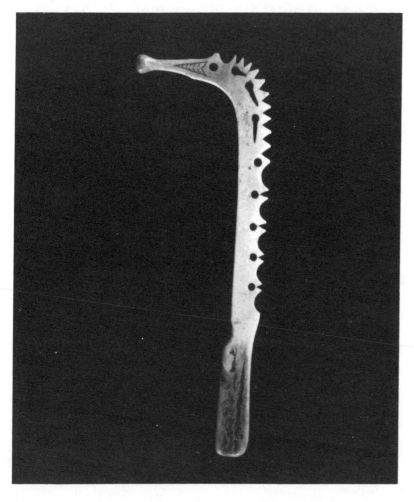

Indian people made things that were both useful and beautiful. This drumstick was made by an Ojibwa person.

The Ottawa

Long before people from Europe came to the Michigan area, Indian tribes exchanged goods with each other. The tribe especially well-known for trading was the Ottawa. Often Ottawa men could be seen traveling with their canoes loaded with trade goods. They exchanged things like corn, tobacco, and woven mats for pottery, shells, and paints or dyes.

In the 1600's traders from France began coming to the area around the Great Lakes. That made trading even more important to the Ottawas. They gave the French furs and food. In return the French gave the Ottawas guns, beads, kettles, and brandy. The Ottawas traded the French goods with other tribes. These tribes then gave the Ottawas more furs so that they could go back to the French and begin trading again. It was as important for young Ottawas to learn good business skills as it was for them to learn to hunt and fish.

The Ottawas dressed much like Indians from other tribes in the Michigan area. In warm seasons the men wore only breechcloths* and moccasins. When cooler days arrived they wore leggings, a kind of pant. Women wore different types of dresses, shirts, and skirts. Sometimes they also wore leggings. Clothes were usually made of deerskin. Jackets and robes of fur were worn during cold weather.

In one way Ottawa men looked different from other Indians. One of the first French people who came to the area called the Ottawas "a nation of raised hair." Another Frenchman said the Ottawas had "hair like a brush turned up." Neither the Ojibwa or Potawatomi cut their hair in this brush fashion.

Ottawa men and women dressed much like other Indians in the Michigan area. Their clothes were usually made from deerskins.

During the 1700's the Ottawa Indians lived in villages along Lake Michigan (see the map on page 29). Their homes were called longhouses and usually had barrel-shaped roofs. Longhouses were like apartment houses with several families living in them. The Ottawas often built log walls around their villages like forts. This was probably to protect the older men, women, and children who were left alone much of the time.

When the Ottawa men were not off trading, they left the village to hunt and fish. Sometimes these trips took them as far as 100 miles from their homes. To protect themselves from bad weather, they built small wigwams.

Ottawa women were in charge of growing crops for food. They gathered maple sap in the early spring and berries in the summer. They also were very skillful at weaving. First they gathered cornhusks, cattail leaves, and other reeds. Then they dyed them bright colors and wove them into mats, bags, and baskets. The things they made were useful in everyday life. At the same time they were beautiful.

The Ottawas often built longhouses. Several families usually shared one of these houses.

INDIAN SPORTS AND GAMES

Television shows and movies often show Indians as people who never smile. This is not a true picture. Indians loved to laugh, joke, and have fun. Games and sports were an important part of their lives.

One of the favorite sports of Indians in the Michigan area was called baggatiway.* The French later named it lacrosse. This game was much like hockey and was very rough. Large numbers of players took part. They used a ball made of wood or hardened deerskin. They also used wooden sticks with small, curved nets at the ends. Rules for baggatiway were not exact. Sometimes it was played in an open area about the size of a football field. At other times goals were miles apart!

When Indian people gathered together they enjoyed other sports. They liked to race and see who was best at shooting their bows. They also played snowsnake. In this sport they tried to see who was best at pushing a special wooden stick across the ice or snow.

Many games played by Indian people were ones of chance and luck. There was a game played with dice and a bowl and one played with straws. Bets were often placed on games which made them exciting. Sometimes a game would last several days. Children also enjoyed games. One of them, cat's cradle, is still played today.

Right: a lacrosse stick and ball
Below: Menominee women enjoy a game of lacrosse.

The Potawatomi

In the 1600's there were Potawatomi Indians living in the southwestern part of the Lower Peninsula. It is not certain how long they had lived there. As years passed, groups of Potawatomi people spread out. They lived in what we know today as the Green Bay area of Wisconsin, southern Wisconsin, and northern Indiana and Illinois.

Potawatomi people moved their villages with the seasons. During the warmer months of the year they lived near rivers and lakes. Their homes were usually rounded wigwams covered with woven mats or bark. When winter set in the villages broke up into small groups of families. These groups moved into the forests where hunting was best.

Potawatomi people were not as fond of traveling by water as the Ottawas and Ojibwa. They built dugouts by hollowing out large logs. They also built canoes of elm bark. They used these boats mainly for fishing and traveling short distances.

Farming was important to the Potawatomi, and they raised more of their food than Ottawa or Ojibwa people. In their gardens they grew peas, beans, squash, melons, and corn. They also raised tobacco. When crops were poor, they made flour from beech nuts. Like the other tribes, the Potawatomi picked berries and dug roots of certain plants for food. In late winter they gathered maple sap and made it into sugar.

Like other Indian people, the Potawatomi used roots, plants, and barks of different kinds to make medicines. These first Americans were good at treating sicknesses and injuries. Many of the medicines used today were first discovered by Indians hundreds of years ago.

Indians in the Michigan area made maple sugar from the sap of maple trees. This scene shows Ojibwa women, but it would have looked much the same at a Potawatomi sugar-making camp.

LIVING WITH NATURE

Indians everywhere were experts at living with the natural world around them. In the Michigan area Indians found food in the forests, fields, and swamps. They discovered many secrets about the plant kingdom.

Indian people used many parts of the cattail plant. In spring the pure white shoots of the root were cooked and eaten. Fresh root was used to treat burns or wounds. Indians found that dried, ground root was good for curing stomachaches. When young and green, the spikes* of the cattail were eaten. The yellow pollen or dust on some of the spikes was used as flour. Indian people also dried the long, flat leaves of the cattails and wove them into mats or baskets.

milkweed

Acorns from white or red oak trees were also gathered by Indians in the Michigan area. Ground acorns were used like flour to thicken soup or fry into a kind of pancake. Sometimes acorns were roasted, ground, and dried. Then they were used like coffee.

Milkweed was another plant that was valuable to Indian people. When regular or swamp milkweed blossomed, it was picked and eaten much like asparagus. It was also used in soup or mixed with cornmeal. Tea was made from milkweed roots and used for medicine.

Indian children did not wake up in the morning and open a box of cereal. But they might have blueberries, dried like raisins and mixed with crushed corn. On top would be maple sugar. Indian children learned at an early age to look forward to each season with its special foods from nature.

Cattail

The greatest problems of sickness came to the Indian people after explorers, traders, and settlers began coming from Europe. They brought sicknesses like smallpox* and measles that were new to Indians. Not even the best Indian doctors could stop the new sicknesses. They swept through their villages like terrible fires, killing thousands of men, women, and children.

The Potawatomi, like other tribes in the Michigan area, had ways of caring for each other even in times of trouble and hardship. The children called their own father and their father's brothers all by the name of "father." "Mother" was the word used for a child's real

This Potawatomi man who lived about 1600, was drawn according to some studies made by archaeologists.

mother and also the mother's sisters. Pota-watomi children, then, had many brothers and sisters and several parents. This kind of family kept the children from being alone. They always had someone to love and care for them.

Other Indian tribes

Among the smaller groups of Indian people who lived in what is now Michigan were the Hurons. The Hurons came from what is presently New York State. They were driven out after a long struggle with a powerful tribe known as the Iroquois (EAR o qoy). Battles took place between the two for more than 100 years. During this time the size of the Huron tribe grew smaller and smaller.

Some Huron people wanted to escape from the Iroquois. They went to live near the Straits of Mackinac which divides Michigan's Upper and Lower Peninsulas. Later they moved to the Detroit area. These Hurons were called Wyandottes.

The Hurons were much like their enemies, the Iroquois. The two tribes of people spoke languages that were much the same. They both lived in longhouses. Many Huron men had hairstyles like Iroquois men. They pulled out their hair except for a narrow strip that stretched across the top of the head from the forehead to the neck.

Huron men traveled during much of the spring, summer, and fall seasons, trading goods with other Indian people. They also went to their favorite hunting and fishing areas. They dried the meat and fish for their families to eat during the long winter.

Huron women worked in their gardens while the men were away. They raised corn, squash, sunflowers, and beans. They also gathered foods like wild grapes and acorns. In the winter families were together again in large villages. They enjoyed games and dances and ate the foods they had stored.

The Miami Indians lived in what is now the southwestern corner of Michigan. There was also a Miami settlement in the Detroit area. Miami villages were lasting ones. Although many families left for winter hunts, older men and women lived in the villages all through the year. Farming was very important to the Miami, and they raised many types of crops. Both men and women took part in the harvesting. They stored their crops in pits in the ground to keep them through the winter.

Both Indian men and women used bags to carry things they needed. This bag, made by a Huron Indian, is decorated with moosehair and porcupine quills.

Menominee

Ojibwa

Ojibwa

Ottawa

Huron

Potawatomi

Miami

General areas
where
Michigan's
Indian tribes
lived at different
times in history.

The Menominee Indians lived in what is now the western part of the Upper Peninsula and northern Wisconsin. These people depended on wild rice for much of their food. They also kept gardens, hunted, and fished for large fish called sturgeon. Early explorers and fur traders from Europe admired the Menominees and called them a handsome, peaceful people.

Another group of Indians who lived in the Michigan area were the Mascoutens. Little is known about these people. An Ottawa story calls them Mush-co-desh and says they once lived in what is now the northern part of the Lower Peninsula. The Mascoutens were peaceful people and friends of the Ottawas. Still, they did not like the way that Ottawa people sometimes fought with other tribes. The story says that one day some Ottawas stopped at the Mascouten village. They had just lost a battle and hoped their friends would share their sorrow. But the Mascoutens were not sad. Instead some of them laughed and blamed the Ottawas for fighting. The Ottawas left in anger.

A short time later Ottawa Indians attacked the Mascouten village by surprise. Nearly all the Mascoutens were killed. The few that escaped moved southward. Some years later they were attacked again by Ottawas. After this attack an even smaller number of Mascoutens remained. It is believed they joined the Kickapoo tribe outside the Michigan area.

There is a good chance that the Ottawa story may be true. Experts still do not have many facts about the Mascoutens. Perhaps their real story is one that has been lost forever in the past.

Sharing ideas

The Indian tribes who lived in the Michigan area were different in some ways, but they shared certain ideas. They believed their leaders, or chiefs, should listen to the thoughts and feelings of everyone. Then they were to act wisely and carefully. A chief was not a powerful ruler who told everyone what to think and do.

Indian people were not selfish. If one family had food, everyone had food. They did not have to lock up their wigwams and belongings. Stealing was not a problem.

FIRE-FLY SONG

Flitting white-fire insects!
Wandering small fire beasts!
Wave little stars about my bed!
Weave little stars into my sleep!
Come, little dancing white-fire bug,
Come, little flitting white-fire beast!
Light me with your white-flame magic,
Your little star-torch.

from *Ojibwa Songs*
H. H. Schoolcraft & Charles Fenno Hoffman

Indian people shared strong religious feelings. They believed that the earth was the mother or maker of all things, from the smallest bug to the tallest tree or wisest chief. Each plant, animal, or human had a reason for its life and needed the other. A bee, for example, depended on a flower for its food. A bear depended on the bee's honey. An Indian needed the bear's meat for food and its warm fur for robes. As time went by, all returned to earth where life began again. Because of this belief, Indians honored all of nature.

The Indian feelings about nature were very different from settlers who came to America from Europe. Indians thought it was wrong to kill more animals than were needed. They did not believe in wasting any part of an animal they killed. For example, one deer gave them food, skin for making clothes, and antlers for needles and tools. Settlers usually did not make use of all the animals they killed. They might take only the fur and leave the meat to rot, or eat the meat and throw away the skins. Indians disliked settlers for cutting huge forests and plowing large fields. The Indians felt this was bringing great harm to the earth, as well as destroying their hunting grounds.

Indians did not believe in owning land as the settlers did. It was impossible, the Indians thought, for a man or woman to own the land. They felt that the land, like the sun and the sky, belonged to all.

Settlers did not understand Indian beliefs. Most of them did not even care. They felt the Indians were wasting good land that could be used for farms and towns. Settlers who did care thought the Indians should change their beliefs and learn to live and think like white people. And so, the people who came to America from Europe stood for more than just a danger to Indian land. Their coming was a danger to the whole Indian way of life.

Indian people honored all of nature. They believed each plant, animal, and person had a reason for its life and needed the other.

NE-NAW-BO-ZHOO & THE GIANT FISH

Many Indian stories tell about Ne-naw-bo-zhoo.* In many ways Ne-naw-bo-zhoo was like a clown, full of fun and tricks. But he was not always up to mischief. He could use his magic to help Indian people.

A story tells that once a great fish lived in one of Michigan's lakes. The fish caused Indian people much sadness. When he was feeling grumpy (and that was often), he chased Indians who crossed the lake in their canoes. Then he swallowed them, canoe and all, as if they were no more than a little clam in a shell.

Ne-naw-bo-zhoo decided that the fish was causing too much fear and sorrow and boldly paddled his canoe onto the lake. As he paddled he sang a song, daring the fish to swallow him. Finally, the giant fish could stand it no longer. He swallowed Ne-naw-bo-zhoo in one mighty gulp!

It was a terrible fall down into the stomach of the huge fish. But Ne-naw-bo-zhoo was now where he wished to be. With weapons he had carried, he began battling the fish from inside its stomach. In great pain, the fish threw itself upon the shore and died. The great and good Indian clown climbed out of the fish and went home.

That evening Ne-naw-bo-zhoo sat in front of the fire and smoked his pipe. He was pleased with his day's adventure. At last the Indian people would be safe from the fish's mighty swallow.

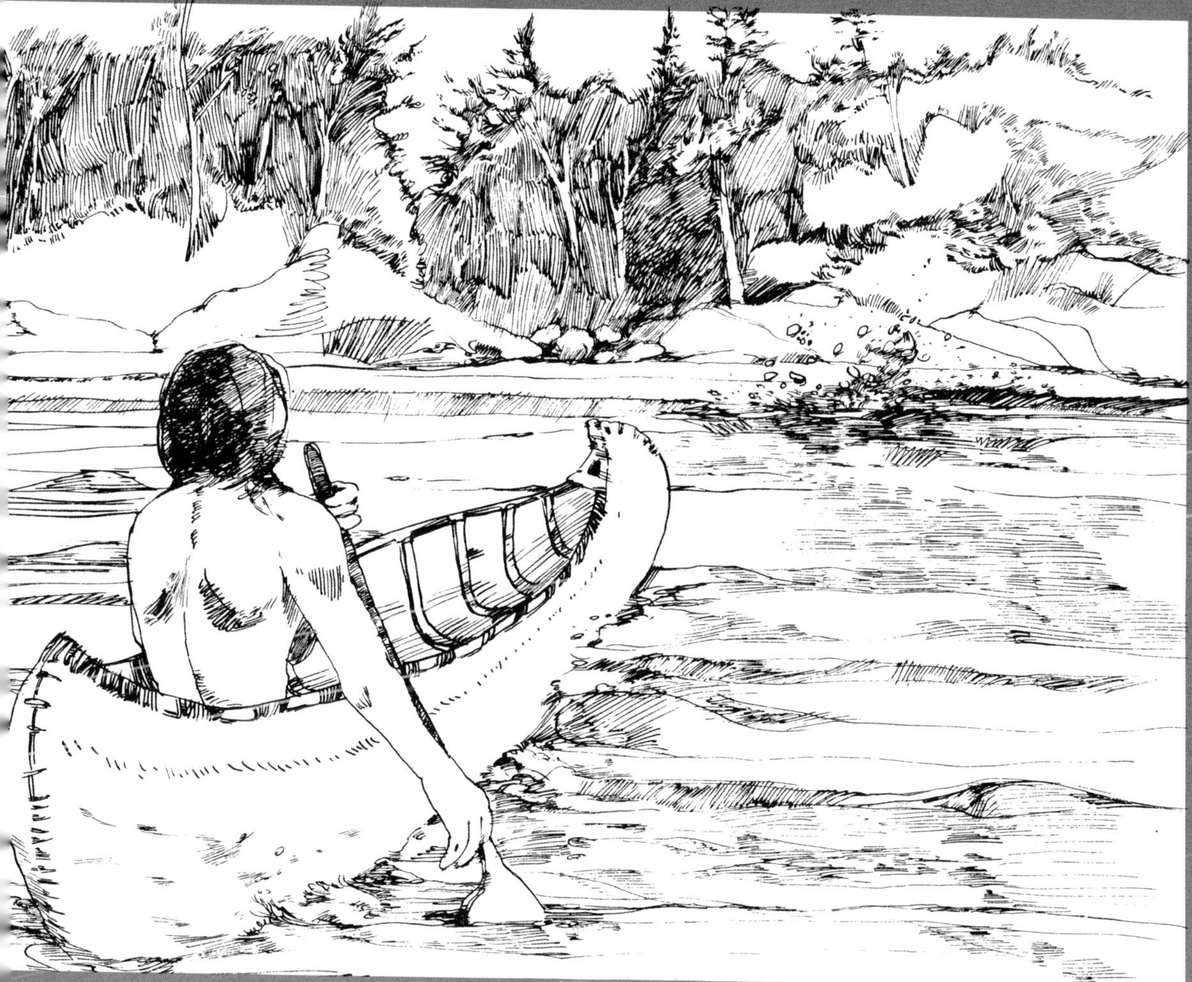

Indian life changes

After traders arrived from Europe, life began to change for Indians in the Michigan area. The traders wanted beaver fur and other animal skins to take back to Europe and sell for high prices. These traders quickly discovered that the Indians were expert hunters and trappers who could supply them with many furs. At the same time, the Indians were very interested in goods such as guns, beads, and iron cooking pots that the traders brought with them. This new exchange between the traders and Indians was the beginning of the fur trade that lasted about sixty years.

The Indians of every tribe in the Michigan area began to depend on the fur trade. Indian men liked the tools and weapons brought by the traders and no longer made their own. Indian women began to use cloth from the traders instead of preparing animal skins for clothing. Even some of their food came from the traders instead of their own gardens.

Traders also brought alcohol, like whiskey, brandy, and rum to give to the Indians. Indian people had never had these kinds of drinks. For some of them alcohol soon became a problem. They drank too much and made poor trades. There was stealing, fighting, and other kinds of trouble that had not been a part of life in Indian villages before the traders came.

As years passed, many of the animals used for fur were killed. Then there was nothing left for Indian people to trade for the goods they needed. Many of them had forgotten how to make these things. Their way of life had been changed forever by the fur trade.

Today's famous Mackinac Island was an early trading center for the Indians, French, and British. It also had an important fort. This drawing was done about 1812.

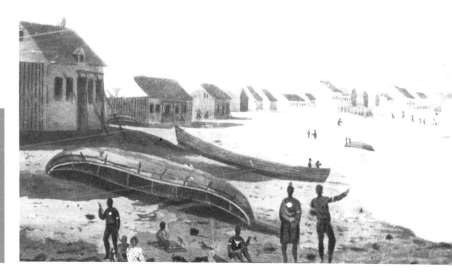

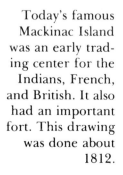

Indians lose their lands

The end of fur trading was not the only problem faced by the Indian people. Over a number of years the French, British, and finally the American soldiers fought to take over the Michigan area. At first the Indian people took the side of the French who had been the most friendly to them. After the French were defeated by the British, the Indians took the side of the British who then fought against the Americans. The Indian people knew that if the Americans took over the Michigan area, settlers would rush in and take the land.

In 1813 the United States armies defeated the British soldiers at a Detroit fort. A few years later the Americans won a larger area that included most of the present-day Michigan. Just as the Indians feared, settlers began moving in. They cut down forests and started building cabins, farms, and towns.

To protect the settlers, leaders in the United States government worked quickly to make treaties* with the Indians. In 1821 a treaty gave all the present state south of the Grand River to the government. In 1836 another treaty gave all the land north of the Grand River to the government. After the treaties were made, settlers could live almost anywhere in the Michigan area.

The treaties said that the Indians were to be given money each year in return for their land. A blacksmith,* teacher, and farmer were supposed to teach them to live like white people. The Michigan treaties, like other Indian treaties, were broken in a number of ways. Sometimes Indians were not paid. When they did get the money, there were always people waiting to cheat them and take it away.

INDIAN LEADERS

Pontiac, an Ottawa chief who lived in the 1700s, united many tribes from the Great Lakes southward. He hoped to drive British soldiers back to what is now the eastern part of the United States and keep settlers off Indian land. For about six months he and his men surrounded Fort Detroit,* which was very important to the British. Pontiac became famous for his leadership and his plan, even though he finally failed to force the British from Fort Detroit.

Andrew J. Blackbird, an Ottawa Indian, lived in the area of Harbor Springs along northern Lake Michigan. He went to school in Ypsilanti* and in 1887 wrote a book called *The History of the Ottawa and Chippewa Indians of Michigan*. He tried to show that non-Indian writers made many mistakes

Far left: Pontiac
Below: Blackbird

when they wrote about Indian life and history.

Leopold Pokagon, chief of a band of Potawatomi Indians in southwestern Michigan, was able to keep his people from being forced westward. However, he had to give up the village that was home for him and 250 of his people. As he signed a treaty that turned the village over to the government, tears ran down his cheeks. "I would rather die than do this," he is reported as saying.

Simon Pokagon, a son of Leopold Pokagon, went to college and was very well thought of by both Indian and non-Indian people. He worked to help his people accept the changing world around them. He also made sure they were paid the money owed them by the government. Simon was well-known for his writing, which included poems and songs.

Below: Leopold Pokagon
Far right: Simon Pokagon

In 1830 President Andrew Jackson and other government leaders worked to pass a law that would move all Indians west of the Mississippi River. They wanted to give settlers even more land for homes and farms. Indians in many parts of the United States suffered greatly because of this law. In the Michigan area it was the Potawatomi and the Wyandottes who were hurt the most. They lived in good farm country which the settlers wanted for themselves. Soldiers came with guns and marched the Indian people out of their homes.

The Indians who were pushed out of their homes had no choice but to go to reservations, or land set aside for them. These reservations were far away in Kansas and Oklahoma. Usually the reservations were poor farming lands that settlers did not want. Some reservations were also set aside in the Michigan area.

Even on reservations Indian people could not live like they wanted to. A government office called the B.I.A. (Bureau of Indian Affairs) made many rules and did not let the Indian people direct their own lives. It was against the law for Indian people to speak their own language or believe in their religion. Indian children were often sent away from their families to go to school. The government did everything possible to make Indian people forget the past and live, talk, and dress like white people.

One Indian chief named Cobmoosa talked about the sadness of moving and changing his life when he went to a reservation in the north. He said: "I am an Indian, and can be nothing else. . . . I know that my people must adopt (your ways) or die. But I cannot change. The young can adopt new ways; the old cannot. I shall soon pass away, living and dying an Indian. You can bend the young tree, but not the old oak."

Indian life today

More than 100 years have passed since Indians were sent to live on reservations. Life for Indian people during these years has not been easy. On reservations there were few ways for them to earn a living. Most of the land was not good for farming, and there were no longer many animals to hunt like there had been in the past. There was little money for food, and many Indian people suffered from poor health. When food and other supplies were sent to them, they were often cheated out of it.

In the 1940's many Indians left the reservations. A large number of men became soldiers and fought in World War II. Other Indian men and women went to cities where workers were greatly needed. After the war many Indian people stayed in the cities where there were jobs.

It was difficult for Indian people to get used to life in crowded cities. They were often lonesome for the peacefulness and beauty of nature and for families and friends. Many of them had little or no schooling and could only get jobs with low pay. Employers were sometimes unfair to Indians and favored white workers. With little money, Indians found it hard to find good places to live. They could not buy the food, clothes, and other things they needed. It was easy for them to give up trying to make their lives better in a world that seemed to be against them.

Dancing was an important part of Indian life. Today it is still taught at Native American centers.

MICHIGAN COUNTIES WITH INDIAN NAMES

Twenty-eight of Michigan's eighty-four counties have Indian names. They are:

1. <u>Keweenaw</u> (KEY wa naw) could mean a "place where a canoe cannot travel and has to be carried." It might also mean a "bend," or a place to go around.
2. <u>Ontonagon</u> (on ton AH gun) is thought to come from an Ojibwa word meaning "bowl."
3. <u>Gogebic</u> (go GEE bik) is an Indian word, but its meaning is uncertain.
4. <u>Menominee</u> is a tribe of Indian people. Their name means "wild rice people."
5. <u>Mackinac</u> (MACK in awe) comes from the word Michilimackinac, but people do not agree on its meaning.
6. <u>Chippewa</u> is another word for Ojibwa, an Indian tribe.
7. <u>Cheboygan</u> (she BOY gun) probably means "big pipe."
8. <u>Otsego</u> (ot SEE go) is a Mohawk* word meaning "clear water."
9. <u>Leelanau</u> (LEE la naw) is an Indian girl in an Ojibwa story.
10. <u>Kalkaska</u> (kal KAS ka) may be an Ojibwa word meaning "burned over."
11. <u>Manistee</u> (man is TEE) may have been an Indian word for "small island in a river."
12. <u>Missaukee</u> (mi SAW kee) was an Ottawa chief. His name meant "great land."
13. <u>Ogemaw</u> (OH ga maw) is an Ojibwa word for "chief."
14. <u>Iosco</u> (eye AH skoe) is a Ottawa hero in a legend.
15. <u>Osceola</u> (ah see OH la) was a well-known Seminole* Indian leader.
16. <u>Newaygo</u> (new AY go) was the name of both an Ojibwa chief and an Ottawa chief.
17. <u>Mecosta</u> (ma KA sta) was a Potawatomi chief whose name meant "young bear" or "bear's head."
18. <u>Muskegon</u> (muss KEY gun) is an Ojibwa word for "swamp or marsh place."

19. <u>Saginaw</u> may mean "place of the Sauk* Indians" or "outlet of a river."

20. <u>Huron</u> is an Indian tribe.

21. <u>Sanilac</u> (SAN ill lack) was a Wyandotte chief in a poem written in 1832 and famous at that time.

22. <u>Ottawa</u> is an Indian tribe.

23. <u>Shiawassee</u> (shy a WAH see) means a "river that twists and turns."

24. <u>Genesee</u> (JE ne SEE) is a Seneca* word meaning "beautiful valley."

25. <u>Allegan</u> (AL le gan) may have been a very, very old Indian tribe.

26. <u>Kalamazoo</u> (KAL a ma ZOO) may mean "runs fast."

27. <u>Washtenaw</u> (WASH te naw) may mean a "river that runs far from a larger body of water."

28. <u>Lenawee</u> (LE na wee) means "man" or "people."

Even though problems remain for Indian people today, important steps have been taken in the last few years. Everywhere in the United States Indians have worked to make changes. They have protested in many ways. Indian leaders have taken problems to courts of law. Some changes in laws have been made to help Indians take charge of their own people. In Michigan Indians proved in a court of law that they have a right to earn a living by fishing with nets in Lake Michigan. This right was one of the few left to them by an old treaty.

Native American centers help Indian people learn about the past and take pride in being Indian.

Today Indians are often called Native Americans. This is to help everyone remember that Indians were the only people in this land for thousands of years. Few of Michigan's Native Americans still live on reservations. Most live in towns and cities in all parts of the state. They have jobs in offices and factories. Some are store owners, builders, nurses, teachers, lawyers, and artists. They live, work, and play like everyone else.

Many Native Americans are working together to help each other. In some towns and cities there are centers where Native Americans can get help finding jobs or solving problems. There is also help for students who are having trouble with their schoolwork.

Native American centers help Native Americans of all ages take pride in being Indian. Some of these centers have classes on Indian arts and crafts. Leaders teach Indian languages or dances. They also tell stories that were told hundreds and hundreds of years ago.

The Nishnawbe story is not one that ends. It goes on as Native American people work together to save the best from their past. It is a story alive with important ideas, like protecting the water, land, plants, and animals around us. It shows how sad life can be when a people's ideas, property, and lives are not honored by another group of people. Nishnawbe is a story that teaches lessons we should never forget.

GLOSSARY

baggatiway - Indian word for their game we know as lacrosse. It has several spellings, including baggataway and baug-ah-ud-o-way.

blacksmith - a person who heats and hammers iron into shapes, like horseshoes. Blacksmiths were very important in America's history, but there are only a few today.

breechcloth - a piece of clothing worn to cover the area from the hips to the upper leg.

conch - a large seashell shaped something like an ice-cream cone.

famine - a shortage of food that causes many people to die.

Fort Detroit - a tiny city built by the French and surrounded by walls. It was taken over by the British in 1762 and attacked by Pontiac the following year.

glacier - a huge body of ice that moves very slowly.

mammoth - a very large kind of elephant with hairy skin and long curved tusks.

mastodons - a group of furry elephants. There were mastodons of many shapes and sizes.

Mohawk - a tribe of Indian people who lived in what is now New York State. The Mohawks were part of a larger group called the Iroquois.

Ne-naw-bo-zhoo - an Indian hero who appears in many legends. His name is spelled in different ways. This spelling, as well as the story, is based on the writing of Andrew J. Blackbird.

Sauk - an Indian tribe believed to have lived in the Saginaw area very early in history. They also lived in the present states of Wisconsin, Illinois, Iowa, Missouri, Kansas, and Oklahoma.

Seminole - Indians of several different tribes who moved into Florida swamplands in order to escape white settlers.

Seneca - a tribe of Indian people who lived in what is now New York State. The Senecas were part of a larger group called the Iroquois.

smallpox - a serious sickness that spreads from person to person and causes sores on the skin.

spike - the flowering part of the cattail and other kinds of plants.

treaty - a written agreement signed by two or more groups.

Ypsilanti - a city in southeastern Michigan. Andrew Blackbird attended a school there that later became Eastern Michigan University.

INDEX

m - map
p - picture

Kalamazoo, 47; m 47
Kalkaska, 46; m 47
Keweenaw, 46; m 47
Kickapoo, 30

lacrosse, 20-21; p 21
language, 9, 27, 49
Leelanau, 46; m 47
Lenawee, 46; m 47
longhouse, 19, 27; p 19

Mackinac, 27; county 46;
  m 47
mammoth, 3, 4; p 2
Manistee, 46; m 47
maple sap, 14, 19, 23; p 23
Mascouten, 9, 30
mastodon, 3, 4, 11
Mecosta, 46; m 47
medicine, 23, 24-25
Menominee, 9, 30, 49;
  m 29; county 46; m 47
Miami, 9, 28; m 29
Missaukee, 46; m 47
mounds, 5; p 18
Muskegon, 5; county 46;
  m 47

Native American centers,
  49
nature, 32
Newaygo, 46; m 47

Ogemaw, 46; m 47
Ojibwa, 9, 12, 13-16; m 29
Ontonagon, 46; m 47
Otsego, 46; m 47

Ottawa, 9, 12, 17-19, 30;
  m 29; county 47; m 47
Osceola, 46; m 47

Pokagon, Leopold, 41;
  p 41
Pokagon, Simon, 41; p 41
Pontiac, 40; p 41
Potawatomi, 9, 12, 22-26,
  42; m 29
prehistory, 3, 10, 11
problems, 37, 38, 39, 42,
  43, 45, 48

religion, 32
reservations, 42, 43, 45

Saginaw, 5; county 46;
  m 47
Sanilac, 46; m 47.
settlers, 11, 26, 32, 33, 38,
  39, 42
Shiawassee, 47; m 47
sickness, 8, 25, 26
sports, 20-21
stories, 30, 34-35, 49

trade, 6, 17, 27, 36-37
travel, 14, 15, 17, 22
treaties, 39, 48
tribe, 9

United States government,
  39, 42, 43
Washtenaw, 47; m 47
wigwam, 15, 19, 22; p 15
wild rice, 14, 30; p 14
Wyandottes, 27, 42